Through
the Basement of Time

poems by

O. Alan Weltzien

Finishing Line Press
Georgetown, Kentucky

Through
the Basement of Time

Copyright © 2022 by O. Alan Weltzien
ISBN 978-1-64662-842-1 First Edition
All rights reserved under International and Pan-American Copyright Conventions. No part of this book may be reproduced in any manner whatsoever without written permission from the publisher, except in the case of brief quotations embodied in critical articles and reviews.

ACKNOWLEDGMENTS

To my river rat friends who journeyed down the River with me

Publisher: Leah Huete de Maines

Editor: Christen Kincaid

Cover Art: Image by Jonathan Payne

Author Photo: O. Alan Weltzien

Cover Design: Elizabeth Maines McCleavy

Order online: www.finishinglinepress.com
also available on amazon.com

Author inquiries and mail orders:
Finishing Line Press
PO Box 1626
Georgetown, Kentucky 40324
USA

"The river was cut by the world's great flood and runs over rocks from the basement of time."

Norman Maclean, *A River Runs Through It*

I

On a girder
along an arch
under the 1928
Navajo Bridge
a California condor
nests in sharp
relief through our
lenses and I
imagine its wide
arch across Marble
Canyon in flight.

II

Larry, 65, mans the dory.
Bald, soft-voiced, he tells
about his company
in Ecuadoran Amazonas
where he white-watered
for many years.
His calm rides the rapids
as the dory torques,
porpoises right or left,
the hull slaps hard
and the bow passengers
bob and hoot.

III

Summer solstice dawn, 4:30 a.m.,
washes out star-studded night
and I rise. One crew member
fires the gas jet for coffee, a purr
spreads across camp and I take
a seat in the oval of chairs
and still myself amid the quiet.
Crew then rafters stir after
the call: "Hot coffee!" variably
pitched according to individual.

I smell the river, track the scene
which slips its dim clothes
and blushes in early morning
light, loud hues, then pales
in the gathering heat and we
pack, eager for the river.

IV

Know	Kaibab Limestone
The	Toroweap Formation
Canyon's	Coconino Sandstone
History:	Hermit Shale
Study	Supai Formation
Rocks	Redwall Limestone
Made	Muav Limestone
By	Bright Angel Shale
Time	Tapeats Sandstone
Very	Vishnu
Slowly	Schist

We learn the mnemonic from guides
but sometimes forget a slot. We
forget hours but not hunger.
"Very slowly" exposes the pre-Cambrian
basement of time and far above,
closer to us, Bright Angel, twice
as old as Hermit, supports it across
intervening strata as one would
expect from angels, shale on shale.

V

The crew trains us quickly
with overnight river bags
then common gear: two lines
stretch from oarboats
to the cluster, both face
the other but instead
of Virginia reel couples
sashaying, we grab and pass
or gently toss our bags
back
        and
                forth
                back
        and
forth
to the waiting arms
of the oarboat crew member
and we cheer.

VI

Alexa, 36, leads us to ancient Paiute sites used to roast agave. PhD student in cultural anthropology, she explains the sacred ritual. We scan the rough circles of rocks, some missing, the slight depression. Half German, half Korean, she reads stories after breakfast as the crew packs. She roller bladed competitively for five years and rowed for twenty but this is her maiden voyage as head guide. She chooses side hikes, breaks, campsites. She swings loads, pounds her boat anchor in soft sand and her stocky arms and legs flex.

VII

Redwall Cavern curves
like a flattened egg and I walk
to the inner edge where
declining rock meets sand
and shout: my sound check.
With crew we set up bases,

clutch PVC pipe bat, play
sandlot softball where a
roving infielder waves
and throws a lasso to hogtie
the runner. Our whoops bounce
off the low dome when a runner

is roped between bases.
No matter my blasts beyond
second base, I'm caught twice,
grin intact: Little League
without coaches or parents,
with lasso.

VIII

Up the Little Colorado River
we pad, its calcium carbonate
load yielding robin-egg blue
and we squint behind sunglasses.

We tie our PFDs as adult
Depends then slip in, hook
feet into armpits just ahead,
ride gentle rapids in body trains,

twist not to un-couple,
laughter rising to the sky
and we shed decades and bob
along, let's do it again. And again.

IX

Vishnu schist was named by geologist Charles Doolittle Walcott (1894) after the formation called Vishnu Temple (7533')

The Inner Canyon opens,
an uneven zipper pulled apart,
and in the basement Vishnu
schist and Zoroaster granite,
charcoal and pink-flecked,
dominate the reduced color
palette, nearly 2,000,000,000
years old: zeros beyond our ken.

In Powell's Granite Gorge streaks
of Zoroaster intrude in Vishnu's
dark mass where wind and water
polish so that patches gleam
like obsidian. Pink lines and curves
script an alphabet beyond knowing
from the spiritual leader, Zarathustra,
who promises that good ultimately
prevails over evil: figure to Vishnu's
ground, Persia with India who
protects and sustains us all.

X

Harder for women
who, at river's soft
edge, pull down
pants and squat,
their bodies a hairpin
turn, hanging out.

In the Canyon
we're taught men
grant privacy
not take it,
the gift
of averted gaze.

XI
—for Marty Schoonmaker

On our PFDs on cool sand
we stretch, following Marty's
example and instructions,
and, Canyon yogi, she steps
softly, adjusts a knee or ankle,
whispers encouragement.
I settle deeper on my cushion,
breathe hard. Marty laughs
easily, always takes the extra
hikes, always wants more.

XII
—for Ashley Marshall

You hear the reverberant sound
crescendo then you spot waves
that spike and toss like meringue
tips before hardening, then your
heart speeds with the smooth
surface fan. The guide has already
scouted and picked the line
and you plunge and water pummels

you and drowns out other sounds
but your shouts. In the paddleboat
you lean out, balance on the bucking
bronco and your paddle might move
air but you keep rhythm. Then you
"break on through to the other side,"
shake head and body like a dog,
breathe more steadily, laugh hard.

Below, you raise your paddle
and slap the others, one beaver
tail, study the rapid, laugh again,
search for the best metaphors:
"yeehaw" more than eight seconds?
or a roller coaster's steepest drop,
tightest turns?
When's the next fix?

XIII

We corkscrew up a gentle canyon,
top out, drop to Shinumo Creek
along the North Bass trail
to the plein-air camp museum

beyond the sandstone slab etched
WL VAUGHAN SLAWOE TEX
9-11-1912. Rusting campware
rests along a low plank against

the rock alcove. Alexa has said
"Shinumo," Paiute, means "old
people." Long after Shinumo,
William Bass, mine prospector

and early promoter, built a rim-
to-rim trail and rigged a cable
crossing below the rapid bearing
his name. Alexa tells the story

of long-suffering Ada D. Bass
who stood by her man despite
his drunks and flings and protests
of devotion—common fare.

A 1900 photo shows Bass
with broad mustache, tapering
beard flecked white against
his dark coat. His decades
disappear before the old time
of the Havasupai he befriended.

XIV

Hedgehog

A poor man's saguaro
or maybe a mini-me
along the North Bass trail,
a garden of bouquets
but hedgehog?
Those wobble, keep
predators at bay
but not laughter,
their spikes radial, erect,
a guarding fortress.
But this cactus branches
towards the sky,
a splay of stems
easy on curves
like a candelabra,
a composed cluster
whose arms arc
like a teddy bear's
forelegs, easy ascent
airwards, their shape
a definition of aspiration,
a calm grouping
in a sere land
aspiring to the far sky.

XV

Chad captains the paddleboat. His dark locks match his beard flecking gray. He knows Canyon geology and botany and the best petroglyph sites. At one camp he packs sand, cuts and sluices a waving line, illustrates lava flows from his 3-D model. He tells stories easily, moments from other trips at this spot, you wouldn't believe what happened. Any given rapid changes clothes depending on flow. He tells me I should come on the first trip in spring for the hikes.

In an earlier life he rose through corporate ranks at Bed, Bath, and Beyond but the river called loudly so he saved money, paid his daughter's college tuition and other debts, transferred out stock options, told his supervisors, "You're assholes. I quit."

In winter he's a private ski coach out of Salt Lake City. He'd been named Utah's Ski Coach of the Year. Wasatch Front winters, Canyon summers. Randy, his father, has guided for decades and he's still after it. Chad admits he's booked for a dozen trips in a row, hardly a day off for laundry or girlfriend. In September he'll train his daughter whom the river also calls.

In the paddleboat he schools us rapidly in stroke commands and we ride his commands through rapids. After Lava Rapid he pops a beer, passes it around, smiles.

XVI

Water and Silence in the slots

A

On our sixth morning we stroll up Trinity
Canyon which zigzags less than a mile
then ends where a slip of water
ribbons down a flat rock face.

Folks sit against walls, chatter ceases.
Then Alexa reads a couple of poems
in the near-silence, that runnel a
sibilant accompaniment, and she hands

me a Simon Ortiz collection so I read
one for this scene and Simon's words
settle atop the warm air and if I
strain I still hear them.

B
    —*for Dave Fenimore*

The temperature passes 100 F midday
so we retreat up Blacktail Canyon,
sacred to the Paiute, for siesta.

Eroded Tapeats sandstone curves
and swirls in this slot a half mile
long and our group takes refuge

in the warm shade, sleeps on pads
in sundry nooks within this rock
womb, limbs loose like dreams.

Joel and I repose on a broad shelf
30' above the floor and the canyon
wren's song flits behind our closed eyes.

After nap I pad to the slot's end,
breast stroke the 6' pool, return
to our ledge, and in mid-afternoon's

quiet, time slips more than half
a million years, earth and ourselves
much younger, and Sean strums

an E chord. The group stirs
from a rest stretching eons:
in the beginning was E Major,

then a few tunes. Sean's soft
voice follows his picking and we
return to now. He loans his guitar

to Joel who sits on a sloping
rock and picks rock or blues tunes
Dave accompanies on harmonica

before he cradles the guitar
and launches into Woody Guthrie
songs. I think about silence then music

and we stroll from this slot's sheltering
embrace into the furnace blast of this
day, the hot song of river and wind.

C

We pass the agave roasting site
near Stone Canyon's mouth, thread
far above the first waterfall,
douche under the second's short
runoff, sweet relief from afternoon

heat, sprawl in a shaded alcove.
A few press on to the slot's end,
the pool fed by a curving waterfall
that drums our heads. We lean in,
eagerly baptized.

Clusters of maidenhair fern droop
below Shinumo quartzite and in
the grotto, Hannah, tall lithe guide,
poses, a nymph. We go silent, minutes,
reluctantly quit our wet pocket.

D

The trail switchbacks beside
Deer Creek Falls and edges above
the Narrows, sacred to Southern
Paiute: a topology of colored strata
and wide and narrow curves 100'
deep, and beyond this sculpture

cottonwoods shade the Patio, flat
rock platforms with easy stream access
which invite our ease. But some
follow the path up the drainage
then east uphill to the waterfall
below Dutton Spring. We scramble

up to a seat behind the falls
and its spray almost cools us.
Just below the falls we take
a seat in the shaded Throne Room,
alcove where small shelves of Tapeats
sandstone have been shaped into

thrones, the work of many hands.
Thrones for all comers, at sundry
elevations and angles, and we sit
erect, shed of dust and sweat,
ready to raise our voices and issue
commands, queen or king for an hour.

E

Kanab Creek flows through
wide Kanab Canyon which
winds north out of the Park.
A bighorn ram, ewe and two kids
pause a hundred meters away
and we watch one another.
In a broad bend, Muav limestone

has receded and shaped a long
alcove, perfectly curved, with a flat
stone row or two above the sunshot
creek: viewing platform for small
talk or snacks or sleep. Some follow
Chad around boulders up creek
then east to Whispering Falls:

usual suite of cool pool, grotto,
a runnel at least 100' down flat
stone, hanging gardens, and in
the omphalos we stroke
the pool, pose in grotto, eat, nap,
our dreams abetted by the whisper
of water, the embrace of stone.

XVII
—for Kim Bateman

After a week, our bodies hairier,
dirtier, Kim rests a camp stool
at the river's flat edge, plastic
bottles ready for business.

We take a turn in the seat
and she kneads our scalps
with shampoo, her hands an act
of grace that blesses our heads.

She rinses with cold river,
her fingers squeeze the soap out
and we rise, clean- and clear-
headed despite body dirt,
her easy laughter tingling our ears.

XVIII

In the first days several hover
around the big webbed bags
attached to an oarboat which chill
our stashes of beer cans and wine
boxes, eyes searching for just ours.
But in the Canyon mystery of river
and sand, strangers turn fast
friends and we sit close in the oval
of folding camp chairs, knees touch
and we offer beers or booze.

Water softens wine boxes and I
rescue the bladders, self-appointed
steward and acolyte, execute my
office. I pause before chairs,
press into communicants' cups,
remind new friends *in vino veritas*.
We extend other courtesies
and shed pieces of our adult skin,
turn into playmates. We unscroll,
revert to youth amidst rock's ancient age.

XIX

Sean pulls out the plastic guns and passes them out. He favors a bucket with long rope handle. Afternoons blaze after summer solstice and he sneaks his oarboat into position, his passengers poised for the first volley. In the water fight's frenzy we dance between offense and defense, shout with laughter as ropes of water chill hot skin.

Sean grins. Tall, thin, bearded, thinning hairline, he refinishes boats off-season. A geology major, he translates Canyon geology. During his short lecture about why the Little Colorado is light bright blue I furrow my brow. Evenings on his guitar he sings "The Loose Girl from Palouse" with a lisp. Other chords invite our voices in. He asks us to write a poem, almost everyone participates, and later he sends the anthology around.

His wry humor pulls us like the river. You never know, afternoons, when he'll baptize us in mirth. Sean throws from his bucket with laser precision.

XX

Those 30 hp. motors drone
before and after rapids,
then long rafts rumble
into view, dozens on board
seated in two rows
of identical long-backed
chairs facing out:
mummies with PFDs
in closer formation,
immobile except
for the occasional wave
or beer can, the canyon
behind them beyond
their ken: fast time
in a cleft outside time.
They disappear downriver
and we return
to river music and slow
tempo, breathe softly.

XXI
—for Joel Weltzien

Up Havasu Creek,
another robin eggs
blue, we ride
the plastic donuts
then sit in shallow
water and eat,
in and out of shade,
while Joel, apprentice,
tries to ride
the donut and spin
in place just below
the plunge
over the rock
like Master Sean
who surfs easily
more than eight
seconds but Joel,
heavier, tips
every time then
he scrambles out
and slides again
into the frothy circle.

XXII

At Whitmore Wash
we step through brush
up to sandstone panels
of pictographs dozens
of feet long, study
stick figures, geometric
patterns, animal
and human shapes:
shorthand alphabet
we fail to decode.
I spot an extended
hand, resist laying
on mine, palm
on ochre palm,
pretending to close
a gap as wide
as the Canyon.

XXIII

We camp one night near a group
of classical musicians and in early
evening shadows their strings draw
me beyond our camp's edge.

On our final morning we drift
past their shaded rest stop while
four play Pachelbel's Canon in D
which everyone knows and I'm blessed.

XXIV

We drift lazily in morning heat
tied together while Alexa reads
Richard Flanagan on his beloved
Franklin River in Tasmania,
our window into the crew's
marriage to the Colorado

and our ride through the basement
of time. Then Sean strums "The
Star-Spangled Banner" on this
Fourth of July and we sing
"America the Beautiful"
and our soft voices gather.

XXV

After the Canyon and the goodbyes
Joel and I stop in the Carl Hayden
Visitor Center at Glen Canyon Dam
which reveals a triumphalist story
of water for everyone, an engineering

miracle with no tradeoffs, no monkey
wrenches. From its bold curving windows
I study the stained bathtub ring, Lake
Powell at least 200' down. The curved
white wall disputes our voyage on rafts.

O. Alan Weltzien retired as an English professor in May 2020 after forty years at two colleges in Virginia and Montana. He's published two chapbooks and ten books, which include a memoir, *A Father and an Island* (Lewis-Clark Press, 2008), and three poetry collections, most recently *Rembrandt in the Stairwell* (FootHills Publishing, 2016). These books also include anthologies and a biography devoted to several Montana writers: Rick Bass, Norman Maclean, and Thomas Savage. Weltzien has another chapbook (essay), *When The Smiles Stopped*, forthcoming from FootHills Publishing.

Weltzien was educated at Whitman College (B.A.) and The University of Virginia (M.A., Ph.D.) He has received two Fulbright Fellowships (Poland, 1989-90, and Bulgaria, 1997-98). He's also received two University of Montana International Faculty Awards (Australia, 2003, and France, 2010).

He has lived in southwest Montana for thirty years. He still loves to ski in winter and backpack or scramble peaks in summer. He has climbed most of the Pacific Northwest volcanoes (though he's a lousy climber) and enjoys discovering new spots in Montana's endless backcountry. He's always been obsessed with mountains, particularly volcanoes. In addition, he and his wife, Lynn, travel extensively before and after Covid-19 times. His bucket list keeps growing.

www.ingramcontent.com/pod-product-compliance
Lightning Source LLC
LaVergne TN
LVHW041514070426
835507LV00012B/1561